The Business Woman With **GOD** As Her Financier

Shirley McDonald

"BE PREPARED BE STEADFAST
BE KNOWLEDGEABLE
BE DETERMINED BE STRONG
STAY FOCUSED"

My God has fought and won many battles for me.

The Business Woman
With GOD
As Her Financier

The Business Woman - *With God As Her Financier*

Unless otherwise indicated, all Scripture quotations are taken from the King James Version of the Bible.

Please note, Eagles Eye Press LLC publishing style capitalizes certain pronouns in Scripture that refer to the Father, Son, and Holy Spirit, and may differ from some Bible publishers' style.

ISBN No. 978-0-692-56563-6

Published by Eagles Eye Press LLC
119 SW Rose Garden Lane
Lee's Summit, MO 64064-2806

www.eagleseyepressllc.com

DEDICATION

I dedicate this book to my Strength, Leaning Post, Counselor, Supporter, Supplier, **Financier**, Motivator, Friend, Joy, and "My All in All" the Lord Jesus Christ.

I dedicate this book to my deceased parents who always did all they could to expose us to and prepare us for better things in life even when they couldn't always afford it. They never stopped trying. They never gave up on any of us which is saying an awful lot especially during the times in which they lived. During my childhood, incomes were so low that most people were doing good just to keep food, clothing and shelter for their family large or small. Another important point, the rule of the house was that we all went to church as a family-no exceptions.

If you thought, you could trick them, that was not going to happen. Instead, you most likely cancelled all of your school activities for the week or sometimes two weeks. We soon stop trying.

My deceased Uncle was another great influence in my life. He inspired me to never stop but to continue to reach higher. He was my oldest motivator. I know he would have loved even the idea of me writing this book. I can envision his smiles and his joy at seeing this project realized. From behind the scenes, he would always encourage me. I thank God for that. His positive words meant so much to me during those trying times of getting started in business. That encouragement continued several years into the business – all the way to his departure from this life.

And finally, I dedicate this book to my two children Lester and Nicole. They had no idea how much of their time I used to make a decent life for them. Much of their young life was spent sitting in waiting areas and near the classroom as I continued my college courses to get my Associates degree. They were with me when I started the business as well as when I returned to school to finish my college education. I've tried to make it up to them for dragging them (during their young years) in and out of college lounges as I pursued my education. I've tried to tell, show, and live in a way that they always knew that I truly love them. I am determined to be an example for them.

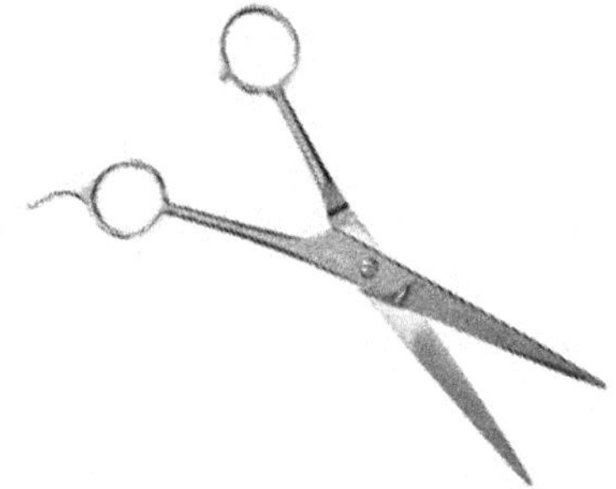

Alumni Remarks: Ms Mac…I appreciate you so much. Your influence has helped make me the man I am!

CONTENTS

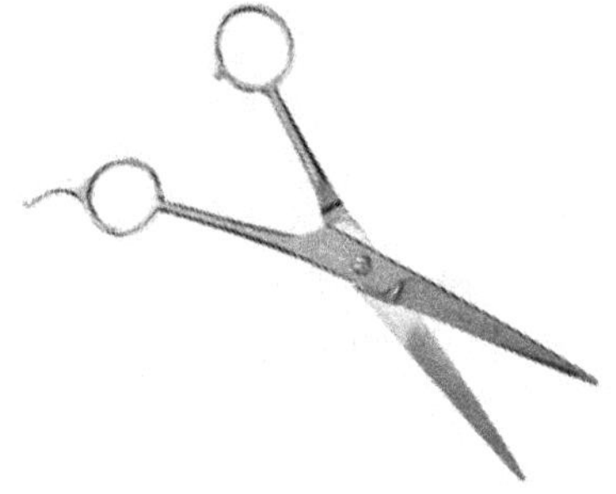

Alumni Remarks: Ms Mac…Thank you so much for all the teaching and encouraging words you gave me, and having the faith when my faith was growing low. I thank you from the bottom of my heart.

FORWARD

I've found nothing more enjoyable over the years than serving God's people. It has not been easy or without challenges. Serving has brought to me a degree of pleasure, joy, peace and contentment, while increasing in wisdom, knowledge and understanding. I started out a number of years ago determined in my heart to help people who had been played down, walked over, pushed back, pushed out, discouraged and disappointed in their dreams, desires or learning disability. It is important not to allow anyone to make you feel inferior or to make you want to give up. Someone cares even though you've made mistakes. People sometimes need to be reminded that we all have sinned and fallen short of God's glory, one way or another. Most of all it is now time for us to unite our forces, pull together, beat the odds and learn that there is strength in numbers. I feel strongly about this. We need to learn to love ourselves first. Really love ourselves! Love and respect for others as well as ourselves will overcome disrespect and dishonor.

We need strong mentors and examples for our young men and women to encourage them instead of criticizing them. They need counseling, guidance and someone to hold them up and help them to be responsible. If they disappoint you, and they will, from time to time, we still cannot give up on them or write them off. Keep in mind everybody is somebody to God. His time was not wasted in His creation of humans. I wrote this book to share my experiences, to counsel, to mentor, to provide guidance and let people know young and old that the impossible is possible with God. Sharing spiritual insight, successes, failures and general knowledge of faith to attain the material things on this earth that God has for us is my purpose. Let us open our eyes and minds to reach a higher level of love, concern and togetherness. Will you be a mentor, an example, tutor or a helper to young people in some meaningful way? If you put forth the effort, God will bless you!

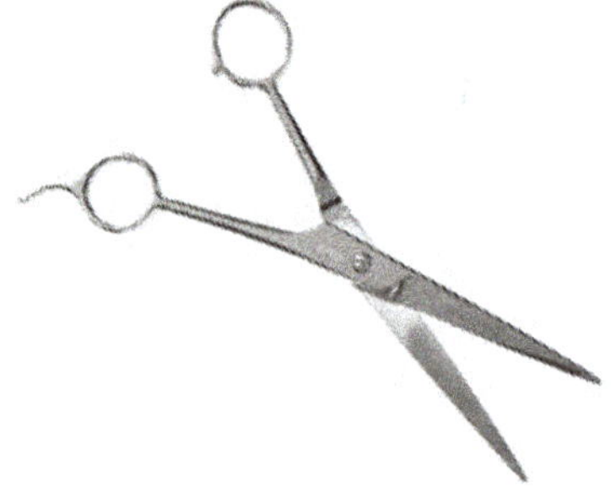

Alumni Remarks: Ms Mac…You have instructing mastered! Not just when it comes to the hair, but you counsel and guide while you teach. I admire you so much. I can never, ever forget you. Thank you.

ACKNOWLEDGEMENT

I thank God for sending people into my life to keep me focused on completing this project. The following wonderful people know the real meaning of helping, encouraging, mentoring, and motivating others in a Godly way:

Usef Harris, a former student and author, was dedicated and determined to organizing this book.

Dr. Stanley Counts tireless belief and continued encouragement help bring this project to fruition.

Minister Rick Lunne a true Man of God in Word and deed. As one of my excellent students, he was one of my staunchest supporters.

Dr. James Terrance (who I affectionately refer to a young man in an old man's body) is my Father in the Gospel. He is a mesmerizing Preacher, teacher, mentor, and example.

Bishop Daniel Jordan prayed for the success of both the School and the Instruction Manual.

Pat Sparks (deceased) believed that I could accomplish this great task. She was eager to tell anyone who would listen about my abilities to reach, teach, and help others.

1
YES YOU CAN

This book is written to encourage and uplift people who may have doubts and fears of ever reaching or seeing their desires, dreams, or visions happen. Some have been told that they do not have what it takes, and are not knowledgeable enough in certain fields. This causes them to doubt their ability to press on and be determined to see their goals, dreams and desires fulfilled.

Keep in mind you are not the first one who has been told this and I assure you, you will not be the last. Most times these negative and false prejudging comments come from those who are close to you or so-called friends. How do I know this? They said it to me!

"The world is full of saboteurs."

Don't allow anyone to sabotage your dreams, plans or anything else. Sometimes this attitude is due to their low self-esteem, low levels of self-motivation, and lack of determination. They seek to turn you around but don't take ownership of their issues. You should take every opportunity to use those negatives to build positives.

Some of us experience these deterrents early in our lives. If we are not especially careful we can destructively use those experiences to hold us back instead of using them as building blocks. Either the experiences will build you up or cause you to fall into a lifetime of doubts and fears.

I am living proof that if God ordained it, He will sustain it. Each chapter in this book provides a roadmap of how that happened in my life. I want you to know and always believe these words **Oh, Yes You Can**. Arise! Shine! Be determined to disarm every negative thing that you have encountered. Tell yourself anything can be conquered, especially with God on your side. If it is going to benefit His people, He will make it work out all right for you and others.

Just think about when the Son of God created this huge world. He did not create it only for His enjoyment but it was for the survival, enjoyment, and reproduction of human, plant and animal life. He was not selfish. He created the flowers of the fields, the rivers and streams to show forth their beauty and what life has to offer us.

"I tell you God is the best example to follow for success."

There should be **no** quitting in reaching our desires, plans, or visions if we follow the map laid out before us. We only have one life to live and we should make it count, not only for ourselves but for others also. Do not allow mistakes, ups and down, blunders or even falls become a stop sign in your life. We all have encountered them, and will always have them because no one is free from it.

There are times you may need to make some alterations in your plans; this is just a part of life. I found that there were many roadblocks not only in writing this book but also in most stages of my life but with God on my side, there was no stopping. I would say to myself, "Oh yes I can and I will." I would memorize **Philippians 4:13**. It says, "*I can do all things through Christ which strengthen me.*" I desire that my legacy be **"She helped those who allowed her to do so. She reached and worked outside the box"**

2
I SAW A NEED

As a young girl around the age of nine or ten years old I noticed my grandmother's hair getting shorter and I saw her mixing up different oils and using it on her head. She had a nice length of hair but I guess she noticed some breakage, and was trying to stop it by using whatever she had concocted. In those days children had to be careful about their conversation with adults and how they presented questions to them. Therefore, I just kept my questions to myself and watched my grandmother. I remember thinking *I am going to find a way to stop or at least slow down whatever caused that problem.* I had very wonderful grandparents growing up and as far as I was concerned, everything in life was good.

My parents were wonderful as well and I thought they had all of the answers I needed. My dad was a very smart man. Some of the older kids in school would tease my siblings and me about my dad being handsome. I only saw that he was there for us and he truly loved his girls. He was the one who helped us with our homework. My dad was the one who taught me by example that not everyone learns the same way. He expected us to catch on to whatever he was teaching after he had explained it one time. If we did not catch on when he thought we should, he had the *switch of education* lying beside him and it seemed that switch had eyes looking and smiling at you. There were times I just could not concentrate on what he was saying and one of the reasons was I was watching that switch.

I decided from my experience with that switch that if I ever taught my children anything, I would never have a switch nearby to use. I decided this option would be used only if I first saw little effort or no interest from them or if I ran out of other means and ways to show them. I've learned that people learn differently; some learn by hearing, some by seeing, some by feeling, some by smelling and many other ways-but not many learn by fear.

It was routine for our dad to ask to hear and see our lesson, making sure that you had worked it out for school the next day. My dad prepared tax returns and did carpentry work. He was also the town barber. Dad was very good in math, so much so that his superiors in the armed services talked to him about studying to be a doctor. I wish he had pursued that career. My mom told us that he was concerned about how beneficial that would be in a small town. He had no desire to leave us or the town anymore. Being a doctor, at that time, would have required him to move the family or for him to travel and perhaps leave the family for long periods of time.

"Mom said what was more important to my dad was staying home and raising his family."

Having been in the armed service away from home for extended periods of times, he decided that leaving his family again was just not an option and not something he wanted to do again.

Mom was a very strong woman. She was somewhat reserved but quietly determined in every sense of the word. If she wanted something done, she would wait patiently for a while and not talk about it to dad anymore. Then one day you would look up and it would be done. If you said anything about it to her, she would laugh quietly about it without explaining the cause and effect. She was somewhat of a jack-of-all-trades. Mom was one who was never afraid to venture out or take chances. She pushed us to be all that we could be. I know she could not afford to do some of the things for us that we wanted but somehow and someway, she would get it done. She was truly a great mother. She was strong, loving, stern, and afraid of nothing. She was a very determined, energetic woman. I have seen her nurse neighbors back to health; feed people that came to our home; and, talk with people who may have been confused or hurting in some way. It seems as if the entire community counted on her for help or support. My siblings and I acquired our determination and self-will from this great woman.

I am not advocating that my parents' way was always the best way, but I can say it did not leave us hungry, homeless or lacking in any way. My parents believed in God and they did not send us to church but the entire family went to church. What you saw them doing there at church was what you saw them doing at home. With both of them deceased now, I still thank God for giving us one of His best couples for parents.

3

TIMES OF PREPARATION

My dad was very protective of us. Before I finished high school dad and I sat down for a father and daughter talk. I always felt very comfortable talking with him. I certainly knew he was my dad but I also saw him as my best friend. I could talk with him about anything, so as I was finishing my high school education I had an idea I wanted to talk to him about. There was so many girls getting pregnant in school, I knew he would love knowing I had thoughts about this and had another plan for success. One day we were talking. I said to him "dad, I will make you a bet." He said, "What is it girl?' He would seldom call us by our name; he would just use the word girl. I made this proposal. If I finished school without becoming pregnant you will send me off to college like my other sisters. He said he would but as I look back in time, I think he was also saying *just make it out of school* and we will cross that bridge when we come to it. I do not think he realized we girls obeyed their teaching about life.

During my senior year, he already had three girls in college. I approached him a few weeks after I finished school. I told him I had won the bet and I was now ready to go off to college. dad was not one to get aroused easily or raise his voice, so he calmly said to me in a low quiet voice, now girl you may have to give your mom and me just a little more time to get things together for you. I said okay. I knew and trusted that he would do what he said. While I was waiting and because I love doing hair so much; (which I had been doing all of my school years), I asked him could I go to cosmetology school? There was not a school nearby so I asked if I could go live with my older brother who was married and was in the Air force in Texas. He was more than willing to say yes to that because he knew that ***was jumping out of the pot into the fire.*** You see my older brother was even more protective of me than dad or mom but now that I am out of school, surely he's not the same. I'm a young adult and I hope he realized it.

I thought my brother would have changed over the years. He hadn't changed even a little bit. I loved my brother and now he has passed on. He had the best personality I believe in our family. He was always joyful, playful and if he had a bad day, you would never know it because of the attitude he carried. When I was in Junior or Senior High school if a boy tried to say anything to me, before I could say a word my brother would get the boy to go with him to walk some other girl home. He would tell him there was something very important he had to show him. It was just one of his tricks to divert the boy's attention from me. I would be so angry with my older brother for doing that, yet I could not tell my mom or dad because they certainly were not going to tell him to stop. If I said anything to my brother about it, with him being older he would just laugh or push me away from him saying go on somewhere little girl. He would never stop laughing. You can see why my dad and mom never worried about me living with him while I went to Beauty School.

I enrolled in Beauty School in Marshall Texas. I enjoyed my time there in school and I might add that I was good and fast in my work. The owner and top instructor called me in the office one day to talk to me about being an instructor and to tell me why they thought I needed to consider becoming an instructor. At that time, I felt good about my work and their confidence in me being an instructor. To start studying for the instructor's course, I took a part time job as a secretary in a funeral home in the evenings to help pay for my training. The funeral home was located across the street from our school. This solved the problem of mom and dad paying for the additional training.

"Little did I realize that this was a time of preparation for what I would be doing for years to come."

I sent a letter home to the family letting them know I would be staying a little longer in Texas, and why.

After working in the funeral home for some time, I wanted to know and see how embalming of bodies was done. I have always been a little curious about things, how they worked and why? The funeral home owners would allow me to see just so much but not the entire procedure.

When the owners went to retrieve a body, I was in the office working alone but any family members that came to make any arrangement changes for their loved ones would have to wait until the directors returned. I was never afraid which was good because I later groomed the deceased hair and found that to be an enjoyable task. This opportunity gave me additional ideas and thoughts on what I could spend the rest of my life doing.

I finished the instructor's course and taught at the Beauty School for several years. After a while, I wanted to do a little more traveling. I wanted to visit one of my Uncles that I had only seen a few times. He lived in Indiana so I wrote him and asked if I could come to stay for a while and he said yes. I went to Indiana not planning to stay, but I liked being there. Dad had always taught us that wherever we lived, the first thing for us to do was to get a job and save our fare back home out of our first paycheck. I did that and started to study for the State Board of cosmetology exam. Within a few weeks, I felt that I was ready and applied to take the exam. I passed the exam. I worked in a very nice upscale salon owned by a brother and sister. The business had a side for barber services as well as beauty services. Everything was nice and as usual, it did not take me very long to build up a consistent clientele. I was there several years and finally got home sick. I wanted to be near my siblings.

I was my parent's curious child. I wanted to know. I remember early in life having my tonsils removed. I asked the doctor before he put me under to let me see my tonsils once he had removed them. I just wanted to see what they looked like for myself. I was curious about their appearance and size, etc. The doctor said he would but he lied to me and he never showed them to me. I have forgotten the excuse he used. I suppose from a young age, I wanted to know how things worked, looked, felt, changed and more.

I noticed many years ago when a person's hair, feet, and teeth are well groomed, their personality seems to be a lot nicer and their outlook on life seems to be a bit more optimistic. To accomplish a great transformation, all one needs is well-groomed hair, teeth and feet, a simple housedress and a pair of normal, medium size earrings. When a well-groomed man puts on a nice clean shirt and pair of nice pressed pants, you will notice how he squares his shoulders and stands tall as if there is an unknown strength in him.

We all know that real beauty comes from the inside and it shows on the outside. If we will just realize how to beautify our inside with God's word, it takes very little for the outside to catch up. Ladies need to be watchful, have their nails cleaned and manicured and keep in mind that little things mean a lot. If you are going to wear nail polish on your fingers or toenails, no chipping, some off and some on. It always looks better if you let your polished nails dry completely. If you do not have the time to polish them and let them dry completely just take it all off. It would look much better.

This reminds me of something my dad used to say when we thought we needed to add extra things to look good. He would say in his quiet low voice, thinking you are looking good and you are looking curious. I personally feel that same way about all of this extra hair females wear; however, I will not say much about wearing too much artificial hair because I realize that is a danger zone in today's world of beauty.

There are real good reasons, needs, and conditions for hairpieces and I thank God that we have them. We need to educate ourselves so that we do not abuse or overuse this blessing. In the field of beauty, you learn that less is more. As the saying goes, little is much when God is in it. Too much of anything is most times worse than too little especially when it comes to beautifying ourselves. We really hide more of our natural beauty than we realize by over using things we think are beautifying us. Just think seriously about this for a few minutes. Sometimes I think we are trying to be or look like movie personalities or the big entertainment figures, not realizing there is a staff of people to prepare them for this special purpose or occasion. Their look is not necessarily for every day ordinary working people and if we feel that it is, remember little is much! I have seen it repeatedly, where ladies are covering up their real beauty by over doing what they hear or see in the name of beauty or style. We really need to understand not every style is for every person. In times past, we could talk a little more freely about what is beauty and what is style, but as stated earlier, that conversation is not so readily accepted in today's society. We live in a do your own thing type of world. I believe in preparing for that special someone with which to spend the rest of my life. What they see should be what they get; however, with this day of artificial everything, we are not sure of what we are getting.

After working in Indiana for some years, I went back home on my vacation. When people discovered I was home, they all wanted their hair done. In a short time, I accumulated a substantial clientele so my dad built a beauty shop adjacent to the family home. I opened my first Beauty Salon. I did have to get an Arkansas cosmetology license before I could work in a Beauty Salon there legally of course, so I completed the steps to attain my cosmetology license for Arkansas. My mom, dad, and the entire town were overjoyed at my return and success. I would work long hours and had very little overhead expense. I had the luxury of doing as I pleased.

In another funeral home not too far from home, I got the experience of doing hair on the deceased and that experience has been very beneficial in a number of ways. The shop that I worked in when my business was slow was near a college campus. My hometown was small and this college town was larger. The ladies in that shop were glad to get more help so we really became close like sisters. One morning the owner of this shop got a call from one of her customer's family members that one of the customers had passed away during the night, and the family wanted her to fix the lady's hair for the funeral. The operator that always did her hair had a real fear of doing the deceased's hair, so she asked the other operator and me if we would do it for her. After a long day working in the shop, we left for the funeral home around five or six o'clock that evening thinking it would not take us long. The wake was the very next day; therefore, we needed to get the hair done that evening or real early the next morning which we would not have been able to do That evening as we entered the funeral home there were workers waiting for us so they could show us around and go into what I called the ***cold room***. This was where the bodies were and where we styled the client's hair. About fifteen minutes into doing the client's hair, all of the lights went out in the funeral home. We were standing on opposite sides of the deceased and I was working on her head, when we heard one of the overseers call out in a loud voice, a fuse has blown. We are going to run out and pick one up, it won't take long. Neither one of us operators even grunted. I didn't feel fearful but I didn't feel comfortable either. I stepped back and braced myself on a table behind me. We couldn't see each other and now as I think about it, we would have really had problems if we would have tried to move toward each other in that pitch black room. That would have been worse than Fred Sanford when he would look toward the sky, grab his chest and say "Elizabeth, I'm coming to join you." I knew the other operator was afraid because she wasn't really eager to do the client's hair anyway.

She had not been our client and the other operator was very nice about coming along with me for support.

The care takers were not gone very long. It was about five minutes or so, and all of the lights were back on. Then one of the men came back to the cold room where we had started working again, and asked if we were all right. Then he said to me, Lady, were you leaning against this table waiting for the lights to come back on? I said yes I was not really looking at him because my mind was on finishing up our work. It was getting late in the evening. I had worked all day and wanted to finish and get some rest. Then he said, "Well I would like to know if you would be interested in doing one more head." Still working, I thought he was just joking. I asked him where the head was. He pulled the sheet back on the table I was leaning against when the lights went out and said "this lady." I turned back around and finished the lady that I was working on. Then I told him **"no"** because it was getting late and we had to be at the shop early for work the next morning. This was homecoming time and we were very busy. Before I could get my answer out good the other operator standing there with me answered with a firm **"no."**

Early that next morning before I had gotten up to get ready for work, the owner of the shop that we were working in called. She explained that the funeral home had called her and said that the lady's hair, that we did last evening, had reverted and had to be done over. She asked if we would go back before coming to the shop. She said that it must have gotten a little warm when the lights had gone out and that was possibly the cause of the hairdo being altered. She also said to me that she had talked with the other operator but she wasn't going back. She was coming straight to the shop. She asked me if I would go back and fix the lady's hair for her. I said yes. I went back and did the client's hair and went to the shop afterwards. I was paid well by the family but the only thing that took me a while to get over was the sanitizing of my hands before and after working on the lady. For some reason my hands felt heavier than usual but that feeling finally went away.

That was an experience that I will always remember and as the years went by it came to me that the lights going out in the funeral home was most likely a prank by those men. I'm sure they thought it was funny but it was not funny to us. I loved doing hair and at the time I thought I would continue doing the deceased's hair on a part time basis or when a family would request the work. When discussing this experience with students I tell them that the dead clients are no problem. They never complain, get upset, never dislike your work or get tired of waiting. Most of them will say, Oh that's OK Ms Mac. We are not interested. We understand they can't hurt you, but they can make you hurt yourself.

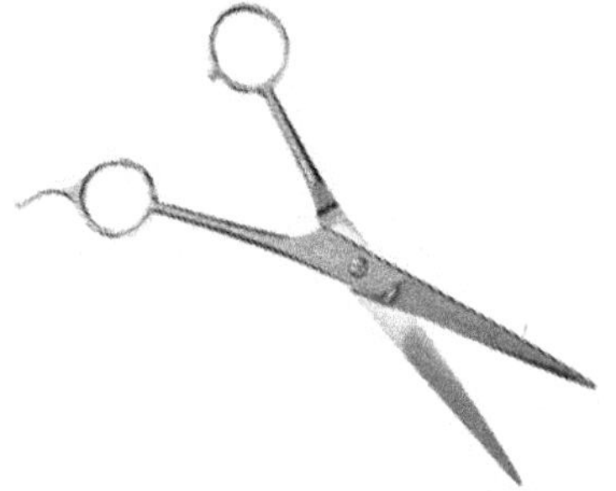

Alumni Remarks: Ms Mac…Thanks for the great insight about life, business, prayers, everything. Thank you so much.

4

GOD TRAINS YOU BEFORE HE SENDS YOU

Several years later I came to Kansas City to visit relatives. This was not unusual because almost every summer when our high school was out for the summer my mom and dad would let us take a two week vacation in Kansas City. I was accustom to visiting Kansas City but I had no plans to ever stay; however, for some unknown reason I stayed. Either it was just time to stay or I was just ready to stop traveling for a while. I had several relatives in Kansas City and I decided to rest from doing hair for a while also. It so happened that a little while lasted for a few years. I worked again as a medical secretary and eventually I felt that I had rested long enough from doing hair. I decided to check with the Missouri State Board of Cosmetology to see what was needed to practice doing hair in the state of Missouri. I found out that I had to take their exam to get an Operator's license and I would have to take a brush-up course to get my instructors license. I met both requirements and got both licenses; however, this was not done at the same time. It took a while. I took my brush-up instructors training at one of the best schools in Kansas City with one of the best teachers I had ever experienced, Ms. Aline Jefferson. She was a really thorough and informative instructor. When she finished teaching there were very few questions to be asked. I liked her methods so much I adopted many as my own. Over the years, I have added a little more of my experiences and techniques because it takes a little more to hold the attention and interest of today's students.

One of the real turning points in my life occurred after I'd been teaching for a while and taught in several schools. I had stopped working in salons and focused solely on teaching. A school called that needed an evening instructor. I was interviewed and hired immediately. Within a few months they needed me on straight days. I guess the word had gotten out about me coming on the day shift. The next morning when I came in, all eyes were on me. It seemed by the students reaction as if they were silently asking me, are you really ready for us? I smiled very big and said, good morning. I heard a few students reply good morning back, but the stares were much stronger than their good morning. I had already seen and experienced this before so it was no surprise; it was even welcomed. Since I was prepared for this, they were not about to take me by surprise.

This was a racially mixed school which was very good for me and very uplifting because there are always students really interested in succeeding. Of course, you have your trouble makers. If the instructor does not stop the game playing from the non-serious students, the end result is an atmosphere of disrespect for the entire school.

I enjoyed my classes and allowed discussion in them, but I remained in control. I have seen instructors pushed to their limits and when this is done you've lost the battle with the students and class rapport. They know from that point on they can distract you and will continue to do so. Every instructor must come to the realization that he or she does not possess all the knowledge in their chosen field and should not pretend to have all of the answers. However, with further research many answers may arise. It is important to be frank with your students and let them know this.

There was one lady on the day shift when I started teaching at this particular school that I watched for two or three weeks not allowing her to see me taking notice of her actions. I could tell that she had been ruling and super-ruling the entire school for some time. She was not an instructor but she was acting out as one. The interesting thing about this young lady was that she was a minister's wife. She had a commanding presence and because of that, people steered clear of her notice me attitude. When I would start class each morning every student was in their seats and ready except her. She would be walking around and it looked to me as if she was inspecting the interior of the building. I would see her but I guess she was waiting or wanting me to call her in to class. The other students were looking to see how I was going to handle this situation. For the first few weeks I ignored her and thought to myself, she must feel real comfortable about passing the state board without studying. The owner was there in the building but she continued to stay out of class. Since the owner was not saying anything to this student, I thought there was no need of me bothering the minister's wife-just let her roll on.

There was a salon on one side of the partition and the school was on the other side. There was a large window for clients to pay for services. From the window you could look over in the school or see in the beauty salon area. This young lady would go over on the salon side in the morning after she had done her inspection walk through and would stand in the window and look over into the classroom where I would be teaching. I finally asked the owner if she was a student or what? He stated in a very soft cunning manner, yes she is a student but in order to have peace in class, I just let her attend when she wants to. I then asked well, how is she preparing for her state exam. He shrugged his shoulders and said that's her problem. So I said nothing else about that. I thought about how that was going to catch up with her later, she didn't realize what she was doing. Not to mention, she was wasting her time and money.

One day, to my surprise, she came to me and asked if she could speak with me for a few minutes and I said oh sure! She proceeded to tell me how she disliked me and what she had been planning to do about it. Keep in mind

"I told you that God trains you before He sends you."

I explained to her that looks are often times deceiving and make sure you understand, steel waters run deep. She might want to do a little more thinking about what she wanted to do. For a short time she continued to go to the other side and look over into the classroom. One day she was over on the salon side but was looking and listening to the teaching. She knew that no one was on the salon side with her and it did not open early; but, she heard someone say clearly, "*touch not my anointed*."

She said she turned around and said WHAT? As she slowly looked around her, there was no one there. She became fearful and came out of the salon and never went back. When she shared this experience with me, I told her that I was glad that she had heard that voice. From that day on she came in the class like everyone else. She went home and told her husband that she wanted him to meet this new instructor the school had hired. She wanted him to come and meet me on her lunch hour which he did.

One day I saw her and a man coming toward my desk. As I stood to greet them, she introduced me to her husband. I could tell what she had been doing at school she was doing in the home. We talked for a short time. They wanted to know the church I attended. I told them and invited them to visit. For a while, they attended our church services regularly. I later lost contact with them but before that time, she had made a real change. She had settled down and there was no more disruptive behavior. I take no real credit for this change; if we will just show people what the word of God says by our actions, I am proof that He will do the rest.

The results of many other cases that I addressed prompted many students and customers to ask me why I was teaching for someone else, when I should be teaching for myself. However, being asked this question still wasn't penetrating my mind, I guess, because I saw an awful lot of good that I could accomplish in this school. I really believed that I was in God's school of learning. When HE was ready for me to open a school, HE spoke to me directly,

"When He first spoke I was not
accustom to hearing His voice
and I refused to accept what I was hearing."

I did not understand that it was ***His*** voice. He knows how, when, and where to get our attention and one day He got mine.

It was hard work preparing an instructor's teaching manual for inspection by the State Board. This book, required before you could sit for the test, had to have every chapter outlined and include step by step documentation of how you were going to teach the subject matter. This was not a book that you were going to be able to hurry up and finish in several weeks unless that's all you were doing all day every day. Every page had to be typed and the book resembled the old Yellow Pages phone book.

I was still working in a salon and finished my book after working on it for approximately two or three months. I'm thinking that it was three weeks before the due date because I was not told the board's deadline date. **BUT GOD!** One day, one of the board members came in the school that I was attending and preparing for my instructors test, to see someone. I had never seen her before but a student told me who she was and that I should talk to her about looking at my book. Reluctantly I talked to her. I figured if anything in my book required revisions she could tell me before I went before the board. She asked me when I was supposed to go to the State Board. I told her I had not been informed yet but I had reported that my book was finished. She went back into the office. I'm not sure of what was said to the administrators in the office but when she came out she said to me, you should have had that book in two weeks ago. You have passed the deadline for turning it in. Call the board and I will verify that I reviewed your book. Ask them to please squeeze you in for the exam if possible.

I got home that evening a little early so I called the board. The State Board told me that I had waited past the time. My book should have been in their office at least two weeks prior! I was disappointed because I had been working so hard on it to beat the deadline. I guess I must have let the date slip by me thinking I would be told about the deadline. The scheduling lady took my name and said that she would contact me if any dates open or someone cancels. There is no guarantee of anything. I was very disappointed and yet there was a little glimmer of hope that something would work out for me. Two days later I received a call telling me to come on a certain day to be squeezed in but it would be on the very last day and hour. They told me not to try to send my instructor's book in because it would not make it in time. I told them that I would bring it down to them. Just bring it with you, was their response. I cannot tell you how I thanked God.

I must say I was well prepared. I even went over time on my teaching and presentation and they did not bother to stop me. Oh, I had lots of material prepared and was ready to present it all. I looked at my watch and when I did I saw some of them smile slightly. I acknowledged that I had gone a little over my time and found a way to close out the session. The board responded with their enjoyment of the session. It took them some time to grade my book. I did not mind waiting, nor did I care how long it took. I was the last person to leave the Board Testing that day. I was just glad my test was over and I felt within myself that God empowered me to do a good job. After an hour or two they came out into the hall where I was waiting. With a smile, one of the members handed me my book, stamped approved. I left the city on a flight back home as pleased and relaxed as a new born child. My real teaching journey was set to begin for many years.

A number of job offers came and I have taught in several places. I was already licensed for Texas, Indiana, and Arkansas.

My mind was made up not to listen to people telling me that I needed to open my own school but *one Sunday that changed.*

Church service was about half way over and it appeared that everyone was really enjoying the preached word and so was I. All of a sudden I was taken out of the crowd into the Spirit as I heard these words, "open a school". I said, Oh No, I cannot *open a school* nor do I have the money to do that. I didn't hear anything else about that and I didn't think anything else about it either. Two or three months passed and again in church I heard the voice say open a school. The response from me again was No. Students are too rebellious and scheming. I never stopped to wonder where that voice came from. So I just brushed it off thinking nothing about it. The next time, perhaps four or five weeks later, I heard this voice again in church. This time, the voice had a little firmness about it and my head went back and lightly bumped the back of the pew. I was somewhat embarrassed. Wondering who might have seen me, I slowly looked around. I did not see anyone looking at me but again I heard that voice, open a school. This time my response was, Okay Lord. This is an awful high mountain to climb, but if you will hold my hand I will climb it. I held both hands up in a sign of surrender. From that time on, ideas would surface-how to pay in advance for furniture, equipment, materials and everything else that would be needed so that at the right time I would have most of the things the business required. Several months earlier I had been told by a lady about an area in need of a school but her voice was not the voice that got my attention. **It was the voice of God which did that.** As I started getting things together for the school, I remembered what this lady had said and tried to contact her. When I did reach her she acted as if she knew nothing about what I was talking about.

"It is our responsibility to stay focused, determined and strong in reaching our desires, plans or visions."

Determined not to turn back, I took control of my destiny and found a place to birth the vision. I found a building and started getting my paper work and catalogue together. I was told to talk with a school owner who had just opened her school about six or seven months earlier and I did. She was the nicest person I had ever met and she was not afraid to help. There were many evenings after work she and I would go to one of the eating places like McDonald's, Wendy's or some of the other places that would be opened late so we could work on legal documents, catalogues, rules, and regulations for the school . God always has a ram in the bush and she was mine. She stood by my side from the first time she heard my voice on the phone having no idea of who I was. That is another reason I am a firm believer in the old saying, you can't judge a book by its cover. I've thought about her so many times since she passed. Often, whether people wanted to hear or not, she would tell about my expertise as an instructor and my good character as a business person. There would be times I would try to quiet her down but to no avail. She was out spoken, very bold and would get pure joy out of seeing my reaction as I would try to have her be a little more reserved.

My mind sometimes goes back to the time GOD first gave me the idea to open a school. I finally realized it was not my own thoughts. I had not told anyone for a long time about the voice that I heard or what I had planned to do. One day the joy subdued my better judgment and I told my best friend thinking she was going to be as elated as I was and even might say Oh Yes, count me in. Did I get the surprise of my life! This was what I heard which floored me and kept me floored for four to six weeks. I had a hard time picking myself up from what was once joy unspeakable. She said I would not do that, everyone knows that (Bam Bam's) school has been the only school around here and everyone has always gone to that school. I just wouldn't do that; no, no I wouldn't do that. Eventually I did recover from that slap on the face. I will never forget that lesson I learned from that experience. When God tells you to do something, you listen carefully, make sure it is the voice of the LORD and do what He say's first then go tell others. Sometime later His Spirit spoke and said, "Don't be upset daughter I did not show her what I showed you, so she can't see it or understand it as you do." When I heard those words I felt renewed in my plan and my determination and got back on track and got the work done.

From that day on I learned to do whatever I plan, desire or hear from Him to do. I need to do that first then go and tell others about it. So I'm saying to you, if God says it, you believe it and that should settle it. Don't get discouraged when the different winds of adversity blow on you from an expected or unexpected source. That could be a teaching lesson for your good. I realize my friend would never have meant me any harm but was just speaking what she saw and felt from her heart. I am so grateful for that lesson. One never knows how a useful lesson may be taught; however, you will sooner or later realize that if God says it and if you can grasp it that is all you need. You must be strong, determined and stay focused. In the Bible **Isaiah** 41:10 says "*Fear thou not; for I am with thee: be thy not dismayed for I am thy God: I will strengthen thee; yea, I will help thee; yea, I will uphold thee with my right hand of righteousness.*" I can tell you that He has done and is still doing this for me. He is willing, ready, able, and waiting to do it for you when you let go and let Him. You must understand nothing takes Him by surprise. He knows where every road block is or is going to be in your pathway but HE has it all under control.

There are times when I think about how God moved stumbling blocks, cleared brush out of my way, picked me up when I had grown weary, and carried me in His bosom when I couldn't find my way. He dried many tears from my eyes, lifted my hung down head when I couldn't figure out the why of things. He counseled me when I felt alone, hurt, and falsely accused. He was the only one there. He never left me alone and I want you to know He is the **real** one there to see about you and your needs. You are never, never to forget that He is able to finance any of His programs. You cannot count totally on people to see you through especially when you really need them. I think even during these times God is still trying to teach us that He is our answer and has all that we need. He can be trusted to see you through no matter what. Keep thinking and saying, "*But God*" and watch Him work it out for you.

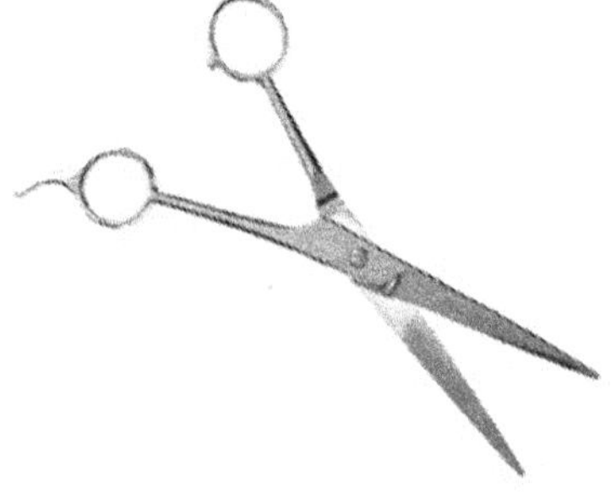

Alumni Remarks: Ms Mac…You are an excellent teacher and role model. May God continue to bless you with strength and know-how ability! Keep up the good work.

5
GOD TOOK WHAT I HAD AND TURNED IT INTO WHAT I NEEDED

As I was preparing for the opening and equipping of my school, I was a divorced mother with two small children and was very careful not to do anything that would cause them to go hungry or without clothing or shelter. God taught me how to watch for places selling things that I would need for the opening of my school. I would look for good used things that could be upholstered, cleaned up or painted.

The main idea was to go in business without a lot of debt over my head if at all possible. Building a business from the ground up is not the easiest thing for ordinary people to do and you can get into huge debt very quickly. However, if it is of God, He can and He will finance His program.

I have also found in most businesses there are slow seasons and regular, or pick up seasons and you are wise to prepare or at least expect those times in order to survive. I am a believer that every place should have what it needs for proper operation but ordinary people do not need to **start** out at the **top**. What I mean is you can be frugal and resourceful by looking for equipment that is lightly used or that can be reconditioned or reinvented.

My dad taught us if you start out at the top, there is only one other way to go because you can't just stay in one place forever. He also taught us one must crawl before he or she walks or runs. I had to crawl first and for a long time. I did not mind because it allowed me to build on a firm foundation. This may not apply to everyone. There are others who may see things differently, and that is ok. Do well for yourself and others. Shortly after I got my first building, adversity and change hit me, and I mean hard. We were in the first building about six years or less when the state bought the building and gave us a short amount of time to relocate. Not an easy job. God had to be in that change. We wanted to stay in the same area because we were growing and the location was convenient for our clientele. The challenge was that the current area did not have any other buildings to satisfy our needs without major renovation. I noticed a large rundown building across the street and was told that it belong to an older gentleman that used to be a builder. I went to the court house and checked it out and I finally found and talked with him. He was interested in selling the building and we settled on a price and since he was doing very little work at the time he asked if I would allow him to do some of the remodeling. After talking and agreeing on a price, the work to be done, and start and finish dates, I felt a little more confident that I might be able to meet the deadline of moving. This man had other ideas. He kept promising that he was going to start and would have the place ready in plenty of time but he never started doing the work he promised. We had already agreed upon the work and I had already put money down and signed a contract with him for the remodeling. I started getting concerned and I contacted him to let him know that our agreement was not going to work because I realized he had no plans to do the work or really sell the building. He was playing a game to get more money and he had a scheme worked out that would prevent my success of opening my business. I had to hurry up and find another place but again God knew the beginning from the end and He worked it out. I had to carry this case to the court to get things settled. When court convened other cases were called and when my name and the builders name were called as I got up from my seat to approach the Judge's bench. I heard a knocking noise coming down the aisle and I turned to make sure that I was not stepping in the path of anyone, to my surprise the builder was coming down the aisle with a blind man's cane bumping each side of the sitting benches as he approached the judge and as I was approaching the judge's bench I stopped and blurted out loud, without thinking about the consequences, "your honor, this man is not blind." You could hear sighs all over the courtroom. We proceeded into litigation and after the Judge heard our case the rest of the case was rightly judged. The case came out in my favor.

"I tell you this again to let you know, if God is for you and the work you do is to help His people then He will be by your side."

He will fight your battle as long as you are doing the right thing and for the right reasons. If God opens the door no man can close it and if He closes a door no man can open it. I am living proof of this fact. We finally ended up in our present location and before we got settled in this place I had been prophesied too that I would have two places. This was something I never looked forward to or even asked for. I think one of the reasons is because I've always liked to pray and have a one-on-one experience with God myself. I'm not saying that He can't get His job done in other ways and I find no fault in other ways of Him reaching His people. In this particular case it proved to be true. For this new move of the Beauty school I saw in a dream, a partition in the school and on top of the partition as I opened the front door I could smell bakery food of all kind sitting on top of the partition. As I walked in, the floor was covered with canned foods and what appeared to be money in all green bill forms. I was puzzled. I couldn't figure out what was going on. I stooped to pick up some of the bills and immediately I heard a voice say, "don't touch". Every bill immediately turned into green cabbage leaves. I believe that was HIS way of letting me know that everything that smells good or even looks good needs to be carefully examined because it may not be good for me. I've always told my students not to chase the dollar but for them to do their work so well that the dollar will chase them. My dad use to tell us that everything that shines is not gold. I am a firm believer of this even to this day. A few weeks later a man that did packets for loans came to see me and was telling me all the reasons I should and could get loans to help my business. He was talking fast and I noticed something about his quick uncertain and nervous smile that did not set well with me. Some of his words such as, it will be like taking candy from a baby, and it's sweet and you being a woman, you can get it, made me uneasy. I said no to him. I believed I could make it just as I was and I didn't want anything that I would have to pay back at that time. That experience took me back to the vision that I had of the sweet smelling bakery items and the cabbage leaves on the floor. One has to be very careful starting out in business not to grab so fast for the get rich quick scheme. Most of the time there is a hidden agenda, especially if your background in business settings is not the strongest. We have been in the same building now for over Thirty-two years and we still have not had to get that packaged loan. I thank God we did not have too however there has been and still are times we could certainly use more money. Wise management of whatever you have is much better than having lots of money and handling it unwisely. To me that is not being a good steward over what God has entrusted you with. I have never heard a rich man say he had too much money but I do know God's word says little is much when he is in it and that is very true because He took what I had and turned it into what I needed.

6

DON'T GIVE UP, DON'T GIVE OUT, DON'T GIVE IN

Shortly after we had moved into a new school district we started to get the feeling that we were not really welcome there. There were things done in a way that would have hurt any young child especially when you know what your child is capable of doing and has good studying habits. I had just been dealing with one of my daughter's teachers who had made a discouraging remark about my daughter's inability to write poetry openly in the classroom which was degrading to her. My daughter called me from the school and was very upset. She explained that she received some bad remarks about her inability to write poetry that day at school. When I was told of the remarks that were said to my daughter it got to me. I told her not to worry about it and we would have it ready the next day. Between short breaks at my school, I began to think and work on different ideas for her poetry project. I know I must have started at least four or five times and would end up tearing up the paper and starting over again until thoughts about the book of Solomon in the bible came to mind and that was all I needed. I will never forget the title, *The Black Rose.* When I finished writing that paper I had her to read and then rewrite it and explain it in her own words, she turned in the assignment the next morning, after the teacher read it, and asked her who helped her, my daughter told her that her mother had helped her to better understand what she had tried to do on her own. Not only did she get a good grade for the paper but was asked to do another one which she did and both papers were displayed on the bulletin board and she also made the Dean's List that year. My daughter was so happy and so was I. I explained to her what some poetry is all about and about the different kinds of poetry. I also had her do sample writings and from then on she was able to do it for herself. I feel that it is a teacher's job to use everything within their means to help children get an understanding of what they can identify with. I feel it is the teacher's duty and responsibility to help the student do this in their own way and to help make sense of any work assigned if need be, especially, if they see and know that the child is trying. There are a lot of teachers that do this and I give credit to them. I believe some are in the business but they do not have a true concern for the children. I will be the first to admit that schools are not the only place this type of action is displayed.

"I certainly believe as leaders we should help people understand the importance of not giving up, giving out or giving in. For young people this is very easy to do."

During this same time I remember belonging to a group of cosmetologists and at that time I was mostly a one man operator in my Beauty School most times. When you are starting out in business and you are a small business you really could not easily borrow money. Because of this you would need to watch every penny and manage your money as wisely as you possibly could for there would be very little left for any kind of help after you paid your bills. Additionally, you need to be in your place of business ninety eight percent of the time. I am a believer that one can assume and move too quickly, take things at face value, feel big too soon; leaving others to do what you should and could have been doing. Sometimes new business owners' start trusting before doing the research of what business is all about because it is certainly more than just being a boss, supervisor, instructor or an overseer of any kind. I along with a committee of other ladies in the cosmetology group had to find someone to speak at a convention in the Better Speakers contest from our state. I was told a few days later that our group had someone and I felt that was good because we no longer had that bother. I remember it was almost the last week or so that our committee was notified that we had to find someone to replace the young lady because she would not be able to attend for some reason. When I received word of this I was also told our group had to find someone else fast because we did not have much time. It was just a day or two after the incident with my child's poetry assignment when we were informed to find another speaker for the Better Speakers contest. I remember racking my brain trying to think of someone who could do the job and who spoke well. All of this time I had the feeling I was over thinking myself and I was tired because I was not the only person trying to come up with someone. I explained this to the students in my school that I was trying to come up with someone to enter the contest and that person had to be a cosmetologist. One of the student in my school said to me, Ms. Mac., why don't you do the speech, you know you can. I looked at her thinking, now you have lost your whole mind, and I told her oh no, I do not have that kind of time. The next day different names for a speech started coming to my mind that would get the audience's attention. A day or two later, I started getting a real feel for a title and everything started slowly falling in place for the speech. I will never forget the name of that speech which was "*Load um up and move um out.*" It was like the right key for the lock. I felt that this was the right title and it was for what I wanted to say. I started writing and repeating the scripture, all things are possible if you will only believe. At the convention, they called for the representative from Missouri. I walked down that long isle to the podium. I intentionally paused for a few seconds after reaching the podium making sure that I had the full attention of the people; then, I said in a very loud voice, *"Load um up and move um out"*. As I went on with my speech there was never a doubt in my mind I knew I had their full attention for the rest of my speech. Most people remember that use to be an old cowboys theme. The verse that kept coming to me as I recalled the student saying, Ms. Mac., you know you can do it, was Philippians 4:13 *"I can do all things through Christ which strengthens me."* I rely heavily on that verse because at first I did not see a way for me to do a good job in representing our state. However, once I started there was no giving up, giving out, or giving in. Our group took first place for the state contest; which allowed me to participate in the National Better Speakers contest; however, I did not see how I could attend that contest. I already knew we were having a family reunion that we were to attend during that same time before I knew of the National Better Speakers contest and I couldn't afford both. One day my mentor came by my school to see me and talk to me about speaking in the contest for the National Better Speakers competition. I told her I wouldn't be able to participate this time and started explaining why. She would not hear anything I was saying and she went on to explain to me what an opportunity this was and if I would just put forth an effort, God would make a way. I do not recall all Ms. Jefferson said to me but I remember her saying, it is past the time to turn in your name but I'm going to turn it in anyway and I will call them and explain the delay to them. I took her at her word and still not knowing how I would be able to afford the trip for my two children and myself, but I started working on the speech. The more I worked on it the better it started to sound to me. The time was drawing near and the speech was becoming clear. In fact I started feeling the moving of the words and I thought even if I can't deliver this speech someone else might be able to do so. As I continued writing, I heard these words, "*You can go.*" I couldn't believe what I was hearing but I kept working on the speech. A day or so later it came to me how I could put things together and make both trips and that is what I did. I figured out that I could be in the speakers contest that evening and my children and I could leave out early the next morning and make it to our family reunion in time. I started packing our clothes for both trips. I remember Ms. Jefferson told me to be sure to have a Red and White outfit which was real good for me because I already had a red blouse and a white skirt that I never really used together before. That outfit came in real handy because I also had a red ball cap to accompany the outfit. When I saw that cap I thought to myself, this is just what I need as I prepared for the speech. Needless to say I felt ready. As we reached Philadelphia we were told our luggage would not arrive until later and we would be notified when it came in perhaps on the next flight. We waited and several more flights came in but no luggage so I got a cab to the hotel after checking and complaining at the desk about my luggage not showing up and we waited for hours for the call that never came. The contest was the next day and I did not realize that my red and white outfit was in the luggage that we were waiting on to come in. I started getting upset however I always kept books with us to read when we traveled to keep the children occupied and I liked motivational books so this particular time I happened to have one of Dr. Robert H. Schuller's books entitled *Tough Times Don't Last Tough People Do.* I started reading that book and my children would said, mom let's pray about the luggage. We prayed and finally I settled down and started trying to believe what I had been reading about tough times. As I was unpacking their clothes from our carry-on luggage trying to hang them up I noticed in one of the pieces underneath their clothes I saw something red. I pulled it out and to my surprise it was my red blouse needless to say I was overjoyed. Then in the other corner of the luggage was my white skirt rolled up. I rolled our clothes so we would have more room because they could only help so much but they were always trying to help me with our luggage. For me to find those clothes really made my day and gave me a boost in my spirit and I felt free to really deliver that speech and that is what I did but before it was time for the real contest I was told by one of our group members that I needed to let them check out my speech before giving it because they did not believe that my first speech was the reason that I won First place in the state contest but It was the way that I spoke. I said o.k. with absolutely no intentions of hearing what she was saying and no intention of allowing them to check anything. Why should I? They had not checked the other one. What they did not know is that all speakers had to go into a room before a committee of people to hear parts of the speech before the real contest and they were not part of that group so I wondered how much checking did I need; God had approved it, what else did I need? All of the speakers were lined up in the hallway waiting for their state to be called. There was a line of nervous ladies trying to express their feelings to each other before they were called, not knowing when our state would be called. When each state was called, you had to walk down a long aisle from the back of the building to the front stage where the judges were seated. I never knew that Ms. Jefferson was one of the judges until I walked upon that stage. She never let me know that she was one of the judges. I still remember when the state of Missouri was called. As I started the long walk to the stage I carried my cap in my hand with the tour tickets which everyone would need (supposedly) to ride the tour bus. I addressed the crowd, judges and proper committee members and then I proceeded to put my cap on and told them their tickets had come and I would be their tour guide. From that point on I felt that I had their full attention for the rest of the speech. As I got into that speech I saw Ms. Jefferson's big smile as she threw her fist into the air which to me meant, keep on keeping on, and with God's Spirit that's what I did. My children ran onstage when I was finished assuring me, along with the crowd, that all was well. I was first told that I had won second place. I wasn't worried about that I was glad to just get it over with and glad that I did not give up, or out. It is amazing what one can do if God is included. The judges or committee had to clear up a few flaws the next day I understand, but we had left Philadelphia and made it home for the reunion the next day when I got word that I had won first place in that contest. I really enjoyed those days because I learned to make the best of family times. It was a learning educational experience while also enjoying our vacation and it worked well for our family. I was again glad that God made a way for me and I did not have to give up, give out or give in to my own ideas. Our ideas, plans or desires are often times not wrong, but we must listen to hear from Him because His way is the best and sure way to most of our accomplishments. Always try Him before you give up, in or out.

7

IF HE OPENED THE DOOR HE CAN KEEP THE DOOR OPENED

I remember when I was trying to study for my barber's license I had to hire a beauty instructor to teach the cosmetology students while I was in barber school. At this time my daughter was still in high school. Every day as I would back out of my driveway I would thank God for allowing me to go to barber school one more day. I was never sure when I would be able to stay at barber school all day or not because some students were always calling me with some kind of complaint that was going on at my school when I was in barber School. It was always something out of order or someone had done something wrong or didn't show up. Sometimes something happened and someone was upset and was leaving class that day. There were few trouble free days for me and neither paper nor time will allow me to name the many problems I encountered while trying to get my license so that I could help others. One day I received a call and they said that the school had been broken into. I was very upset and I told my instructor at the barber school what had happened and that I was going to have to leave and go see about things at my school, he said alright. I left headed toward my school not aware of how fast I might have been going but as I got about half way there I heard a soft quiet voice say, "Daughter, it's not all lost." I remember slowing down and wondering was I really hearing what I thought I heard or was I over thinking myself. Whatever it was it proved to be what I needed and what I thought I heard the first time; one would never believe how many times that door has tried to be closed one way or another (but God!) When I pulled up in front of the school nothing appeared to be wrong, there were no police cars, no people standing around so I cautiously got out of my car and slowly went into the school. Everyone was in their seats but as I entered the room everyone looked at me and everyone was very quiet. No one said a word but the looks were not real fearful looks so I asked, "what happened?' Where was the break in, what was taken, how did they come in? I was asking all of these questions because I did not see anything missing. Nothing was torn up or scattered, the snack machines were still intact. The soft drink machine and water cooler was not touched, so I was asking them and myself what had happened; after a few silent minutes someone spoke up and said they thought they entered through the back door because the police had been there and tested for finger prints on the backdoor. I then went to check the back door exit and there was no sign of forced entry on the inside or outside. However, looking outside down the three or four steps from the porch, I saw one or two hair tapes that had been dropped or left there. The only other signs I noticed was there were some curling irons and maybe a blow dryer or two missing. Well I knew from seeing that what had most likely happened so I did not bother looking any further. I only wanted to thank God, as I remembered that voice as I came down the freeway to the school. Daughter, it's not all lost. This also allowed me to really notice that if God opens a door, He can keep it open and no man can successfully close it. I started looking around that day to find another school that I could attend during the evening hours so that I could be in my school during the day and finish my barber training at night. I called around to several places and was told that I could finish my hours in another barber school in the evening because they offered evening classes. I just needed to bring my credentials and they would do the rest. That evening when I closed the school I found my way to the other school to drop off my credentials and to talk with the people in charge, as I was told what I would have to do. This school was not close to my school nor had I ever been there before. So not only did I have to get someone to drive me there, I had to pay them, only to hear in the end, "we can teach you to cut and give you a certificate because that is all you want to do anyway isn't it?" I said No, and that isn't what I talked with you about before I came here. I was studying for a **license** not a **certificate** and there is a big difference. So since I wouldn't settle for the certificate they started coming up with other excuses. So I had to go back to the drawing board and come up with another plan in order to finish my barbering schooling. I was mighty glad that I had not withdrawn from the first school because I ended up back there. I did not tell the instructor that was working for me that I knew what had happened when the supposed break in happened but I took notice of how she reacted to it as she looked up in the ceiling after all talk had been settled and she said to me, "now what are you going to do with this building?" I said to her, I'm going to have class right now and I do not know what you are going to do. I told the students to get your books out we are going to have class. I never heard a word from them; but, the instructor said, "Well I'm going to leave because I'm too upset." I said, Alright. She left and we never heard from her again. I thought she was just going to be leaving for the rest of that day in order to calm down from the supposed break-in. She was a very nice, low key, well liked and a beautiful person and I really wanted to keep her on. I felt there were a few areas that I could have been a help to her if she wanted me to do so; I never saw or heard from her again. I ended up going through a couple of part time instructors before I made it out of school but this just goes to prove that God can make a way where there is no way. I'm still going on even being semi-retired.

"He can do above and beyond anything we can ask or think."

This should also be proof to real believers that if God opens a door all we have to do is walk there in with faith in Him and watch Him keep that door open for us, only He can. As I stated before, this school was the ***first African American owned barber school*** that I know of in a number of states and certainly in Missouri, at that time (1989). My obeying God by following through what I heard from Him when He said open a school has led to many welfare moms, street walkers, doubters, misunderstood, hurt, disgusted, abandoned, falsely accused, absent mom's and dad's children, jailed and prison men and women lives has been changed. They found a place of acceptance, love, Godly concerned, and discipline. I am regarded as their second mom. Their lives have been turned around for the better. They are now self supportive citizens some went back to college others went into the field of ministry, shop owners and more which proves to me that God is a God of His word when the word says He is no respecter of persons. I am a witness because He has certainly been there for me and is still doing great things for me. He desires to do and be there for you if you will just allow and acknowledge Him faithfully.

8

BIG DREAMS, BIG DESIRES, BIG VISIONS

Dreams, desires and vision, they all have a purpose and a meaning. Don't take them lightly. Have you ever noticed how closely they are related? They can work independently or together. They can help teach you who you are and who you can be and they all have a purpose. I encourage you to study your desires carefully, research your dreams and write your visions. Stay focused on these three. Believe in them. Work toward them. See and feel them. Embrace them and never give up on any of them. Never underestimate them and be determined to conquer at least some of them. I believe that a desire is a state of longing and more. A dream I think of as an aspiration and sometimes it can be a form of prayer, while a vision is something supernaturally perceived or revealed. Be careful not to allow the cares, conditions or situations of this world to dictate the finality of them for you.

"Don't tell the world what you will or can do, show them. Don't believe everything thing they tell you about what can't be done, what's impossible, what's hopeless or that you will not do well in that arena."

You cannot afford to invest in that kind of thinking because God's word says, "*all things are possible, through Christ.*" So who are you going to believe? As you continue studying you will find for yourself that leadership and success most of the time starts with a vision. The Bible declares in Acts 2:17"Your young men will see visions." I once read John F. Kennedy dreamed of putting a man on the moon. Eleanor Roosevelt desired equality for women. Martin Luther King dreamed of betterment for his people. Marva Collins desired to help children that were poverty stricken with little hope of ever doing better. As you can see when you look around, none of these aspirations went without being noticed or carried out in some way. Visions that I had many years ago I still remember today as well as the times that I had them. I remember once in a vision, I saw a very large ship out on the sea. This ship was so overloaded with people that there was very little standing room not to speak of room for moving around. As the ship moved swiftly down the sea toward the safety zone where people were waiting to be taken to a safe place it appeared that the people sailing the ship were loading more and more people in the ship paying no attention to the already overcrowded people in the rear of the ship. You see, this seemed to be a very large one deck ship with the only closed area being a somewhat small area in the front for the men who were in full control of the ship. These men paid no attention to the confusion or yelling going on in the back of the ship and there were many sick, disabled, and older people. Some people fighting, some were being trampled in the floor, some were being pushed over board, and you must understand all of these people were trying to get on board regardless of their conditions. They were of the impression that to get on board meant that they were going to a safe place where they could be helped with their sickness, sorrows, distress, heartaches, weaknesses, hurts of all kinds, and conditions of all kinds only to realize too late that this was not the case and now they were more disappointed than before. In this vision I saw sick people jumping over board, some fell overboard, some were almost dead, and others were dumped overboard. The waters were filled with people some going down for their last time in a fetus position, some bobbing up and down calling for help, some had one hand above the water as if they were trying to show where they were so someone might help before they went completely under. Several yards behind this large ship all of a sudden I saw a number of what I would call small tug boats equipped with all kinds of safety devices and they were throwing them out to the people that could hold on to them. Some of these smaller boats could pull them up close enough to grab some part of them and pull them in to their boats which was a blessing and lifesaving act to many almost lost, hurting and hopeless people. When they were able to express their thanks the one thing most of them would be saying was, "Thank you." Now I believe I will make it to the safety zone to get some help. Before they could even express how thankful they were these men in the small boats were constantly encouraging them saying, that they were now safe and they would make it to the safety zone. It looked as if the tug boats that were helping the people to safety were displaying different names of positive adjectives such as the ***desire*** boat, which was throwing out life lines of all kinds and colors pulling people into his boat saying comforting words to them to help them know that things were better now. The captain of the dream boat was throwing out all kinds of life saving devices even nets in some areas he and his helpers were pulling people into their boat also assuring them that they would make it to the safety zone. Then there was the ***vision*** boat, this captain was helping to save many as he recalled that he had seen this condition in a vision some time ago but certainly did not understand it would have been like this or at this time. After this experience he realized that the Word said the vision is for an appointed time. Now, if you've had a **vision**, **dream**, **desire** or just a plan, this should help you understand you should hold on and never entertain the idea of giving up. Continue working keeping in mind that quitters never win and winners never quit. I found going up a hill is always harder than coming down and if what you are attempting to do has been done before or has not been done at all, remember you can be the first, a game changer or a trend setter. I remember a time I was in a grocery store and a fellow I knew little about but had seen him from time to time, would always start talking to me about music. He had taught music and he knew I loved music and had done a little playing by ear and a little by notes but always wanted to play faster and more efficient than I could read the music. I could hear the sound I wanted but could not really tell you whether it was a major, minor or what before I started reading music. He would suggest to me that I slow down and learn to play it efficiently. Well there was one time after talking to him that was a little different. When I saw him we greeted each other as usual and he started to prophesy to me. I just stood there looking at him as he continued. I had heard some years ago that he sometimes would do this but it was very seldom and we never discussed the subject before. He started telling me that I would own schools and I listened for a while and started laughing quietly saying to him, Now you know that I already own a beauty school, he then said, I did not say a school I said schools. I stopped laughing and started wondering what on earth he could be talking about as he continued telling me much more. I must admit I am not one to look for foretelling of things I have to admit I like hearing from God myself. I'm not saying there is anything wrong with prophesy or a message by others from God by any means but it has always been my desire to hear from Him myself. That way I can really put real trust in to what I hear. I may be this way due to the fact that I have heard that small still voice before and there was no doubt in my mind left to wonder about, and let me say I do know that God has many ways of speaking to us or getting our attention.

"So I'm saying to you, never doubt what God may have said but your job is to pray about it and make sure that it is from God."

I can tell you in my case it was from Him and I was glad about it. You read earlier, in this book, I wrote when He spoke to me and told me to open a school. I certainly did not do it for any other reason nor did I obey the first time I heard the voice because I was not sure it wasn't me out thinking myself nor did it enter my mind about the many friends, students and client's that had approached me with the same suggestion or question. This last voice was one of a kind, it was different and carried with it real power. It truly got my attention that time and I still thank Him. Little did I think, that this was the beginning of a vision I had seen long ago. As I acknowledged Him, I was led by Him every step of the way and He will do the same thing for you if you will hold on to your dream–your desire–your vision.

9

IF GOD DID NOT SAY IT, YOU STILL STAND A GOOD CHANCE

Just before I opened the school I heard "***beware of the three dogs***." I did not understand what this meant but it never left my mind. I am not sure just when the meaning surfaced. I think it had to be within the first one or two years of operation. I experienced all three dogs of course at different times and clearly remember each one, but because I heard it, kept it in my mind and obeyed the warning, I was better able to handle each situation as they came. The name of these three dogs was lust, pride and money, and I will never forget these dogs. Please believe me; they are very detrimental to any business. ***Lust. Pride. Money.*** Sometime Satan will use only one dog and if that one dog can't get the job done he will use two on you. If those two can't get the job done there will be times he will use all three of them on you and the only real dependable hope you have is in Jesus. Now I know many of you will put a question mark by this but just think for a few moments of how many failures in business have happened, and are still doing so today because of lust, pride, and money. Frequently, people in business (not all) feel this is a door opener for them to really use to their advantage and there is little repercussion. You most likely could name a few you either know of, have heard or read of with very little shame. For sure pride is so very easy to slip into and pride will make you feel its presence, making you feel that you have really arrived and this is something you now deserve with no strings attached. Desiring and determined that you make sure to showcase him, pride needs to be seen, heard and praised. Please believe me this is a no, no. In many cases it's a turn off for people. Some weak minded people might put this kind of behavior up front thinking this is the way they would like to be or if they ever get to a point that they feel they can act it out, this is the way they plan to do it. Don't forget the main dominating dog of the three is the money dog. It will lay back and let the other two dogs (lust and pride) have all the time they need to get their job done then he will come out like that male lion from his relaxed and observant corner to show them how the job is to be easily done. Notice it does not take him a long time to get his point over only a few seconds of showing you the Green and how easy it is for you to get a lot of it fast and easy; then, he slowly goes back to his domain leaving you to hunger and chase after him. Do not do it. Let him go. You will appreciate it later.

"I found that God can finance any of His programs and when He chooses to do so, it is well done, stable and trustworthy."

This brings to mind, before I thought about a school of my own; I had been going to college taking a few classes each semester because I had gone through a divorce and my children came first so I couldn't afford to just take off and go to college full time. I had to work to support them and I did not mind doing that so when this opening of a school finally got on my mind I had to drop full time college for part time classes, but as God would have it, the Bible says in Psalms 37:4, "*Delight yourself in the LORD and he will give you the desires of your heart,*" and to finish one day was my desire. I think I had been in business some five or six years or even more. One evening after I had come in from work and the children were doing their school work the evening news came on and I saw a lady on the news, and the News reporters were showing her graduating from college with her grandchildren and she was saying that she was thinking about continuing her education. I think she said she was in her eighties. That's when I said out loud, oh no, that's it. I'm going back and finishing my education this time, and I did. I use to think about that lady and I wondered if she continued her studying and I thought about how she would feel if she only knew how she inspired me to go back and finish my schooling even as I was operating a business and raising two children. That's why I can tell others there is no job too hard for God. There is nothing He can't handle as long as you count on him and do things to help others. I remember that lady said she wanted to teach History on cruise ships. I wasn't quite sure of just what she meant at that time, but later I recall cruising is very educational as well as enjoyable but it also calls for planning. Most people are not fortunate enough to pick up and be able to go any place they desire without planning ahead; especially when they are young and just starting out in the work force. I know there are some who have families with money, there are others who have inherited or won large sums of money; however I'm not sure we can say that is the norm, or I should say it was not so for me.

10

PLANNING AHEAD

By having a solid family foundation, reading, listening to others, attending different classes and lectures I learned the importance of planning. This is especially true when you are in a job setting where you are paid then and there by each client you serve. Sometimes a few one dollar bills in your pocket will make you feel you have done better than you have, not thinking of the many unseen circumstances or emergencies that await you in life. Emergencies and unexpected issues can leave you with anger or disgust and cause you to feel that all of your work has been in vain, which isn't true. When you are young and starting out, you are sometimes unprepared for the when, why, or where to save or invest wisely. You should consider taking classes or reading up on the importance of doing so. No one has to be highly intelligent to notice that you are a Good Dummy. The kind everyone has been waiting for with open arms, one who has not been taught anything about managing finances and has several dollars in his pocket and a few in the bank. Vultures will always be there for he or she who feels they can now live loose or large. Believe me they can tell that you know little or nothing about planning. When this is detected people and THINGS will come crawling out of the woodworks to help you by using you up and when you wake up and understand what has happened most times it's too late.

"I stress to my students the importance of starting small and getting into a habit of being good stewards over whatever God has entrusted with you."

If we would just pay close attention and perhaps slow down our desire to get rich overnight which isn't likely; we would be able to see clearly the many signs of caution that are there for our protection. There was another time I clearly saw in a dream, where there was a glass shelf which measured about 20' x 20' and it was packed with large bills of what looked like $50, $100, $500 and more. I couldn't see all of them even with them being neatly stacked. Then as I stood wondering about where this money came from and who would leave this money out like that, I found that the glass shelf was locked and there was no visible way of unlocking it other than breaking the glass. I finally started looking around in the room at other things and noticed a small room which looked to be about the size of a 9' x 7' room and this room was filled from the floor to the ceiling with bills, but you could not see clearly the denomination of any of the bills which left you like a child looking in the window of a candy store. Then I looked back at that small glass jar of large bills sitting on the counter then back to the room of money trying to choose which one I would like to have. I seemed to also wonder why there was such an uneven amount in the same room anyway. I can't remember how that dream ended but I will never forget the thought it left in my mind. Everything that looks good is not good and little is much when God is in it. Now as years passed I understood that dream a little better because you see in the large room where there was stacks and stacks of money and some of it was just loose in the room all in the floor, I remember I could not see the denomination of any of those bills whereas I could see it in the small glass container. I was left with the feeling that I would rather know what I have or what I am getting into rather than to guess about it any day only to find out later that I had grabbed a fist full of nothing. I have found out through my experience in business, I really had to stay focused, strong and determined. Others may say they did not have to do any of that, but I will tell the world I had to count on God's unchanging hand the best way I knew how to see me through. There were times and there are still times I get disgusted with myself, feeling I haven't done my best or that I have fallen short of what I should have done, but I am so glad that He made a way of escape for all of us. Giving us another chance by repentance, getting up and trying it again and again, careful about discussing it with your friends, family or anyone else. How many times has He had to do this for you? Think about it. You know He deserves all honor, praise and thanksgiving for what He has done for you, what He is doing for you right now and what He will and only He can do for you in the future. Having an A and B plan in business and now I think it would be wise to also have a C plan as well. Keep in mind God is the best business partner you can ever have. He will give you the strength, insight and the ability you will need for the ideas you will need for the job the support you will need, courage and as stated before He can finance any of His programs. God will never be absent from the job. There will never be a time of jealousy, payback, getting even or forsaking you. Now isn't that the kind of business partner you need.

"If God ordained it He will sustain it"

The idea of opening a **barber** school really brought to mind the story of Lydia in the bible in the book of Acst. To me Lydia was a game changer, a Trail blazer and much more because I see her entering into a field dominated heavily by males. I don't recall reading where she encountered any trouble so I guess she must have left it all for me. Lydia was a believer, a business woman, a worshiper, a praying woman and a learner. She was a manufacturer of a purple dye by extracting a white fluid from the veins of shell fish, which to me could have been a very tedious job to say the least. I'm sure some of the shell fish veins were too small or the fluid may not have been as clean or clear as she needed so she had to be very careful in selecting the right shell fish with the right size veins so Lydia as with myself realized at some point that IF GOD ORDAINED IT HE WILL SUSTAIN IT; especially when His light turned that white fluid into beautiful shades of purple and some red's she had to know this was His work for her. I remember He spoke to me ***three*** times before I realized it was His voice that I was hearing and when I finally realized it was Him and I starting obeying as He lead me through the necessary steps and I must admit, I have never regret following His leadership. Now I must tell you just because He called me to go on this mission and He guided me through it. He ordained it and has sustained it. Does not mean it has been free of up's and down's or without trouble. There will be times as you obey God hoping and trying to help His people, the one in most need is the one that will try to bring the business down whether they're aware of it or not. Either way it is due to a degree of ignorance of His word. So when you encounter these kind of situations and please believe me, you will, just hold on to His hand tighter and continue to move forward because He can handle the battle.

11

BARBERING
ANOTHER NEED I SAW

Six or more years after operating the Beauty school I noticed there was not and never had been a barber school in our community, and what was so good about it was that the only barber school close by had been located downtown and little did I know it had moved out. I was told about a year later or even longer that there was a need for a barber school in that area but I was not even aware there was one downtown or had ever been. I guess this was because I never had gone into a barber school as I remember. I would always go to a barbershop for my son to get his hair cut. It never occurred to me that I could get the same result most time cheaper. I only knew that my dad was a barber, one of my mother's brother's and several other males in my family cut hair. Early in my childhood, I remember watching my dad cut men's hair. My dad was one that was not going to allow any of his daughters to come around where he was cutting men's hair and I don't believe even today that he would have ever thought that one of his daughters would have followed his footsteps but perhaps one of his sons. I noticed so many young men walking around on the street looking like they had nothing to do, no place to go, somewhat lost or stuck, nothing to look forward to. I SAW A NEED.

"One thing I do know for sure is that most young people have untold, unknown, undiscovered and unbelievable talents, gifts and abilities that even they are not using or aware they possess."

They are most times far more intelligent than they appear to be or display. An awful lot of times they act out trying to cover up for not doing what they really would like to do. They either have been hurt, disappointed, left out, pushed back in some way or there has been no one to encourage them so they act out as they see others do thinking this is okay or, expected. Acting out means they belong to something or that they have been accepted and someone cares about them. Satan saw and designed a plan and they fell in head first. There are those who might have fallen or somehow lost their way and there is no one in the home to take a real interest in them doing anything constructive and others on the outside not interested enough to give them a chance, helping hand, or show them a better way. Some are simply too concerned about self-satisfaction to care about anyone else. Most times there would only be a mother in the home trying to keep a roof over their head, clothes on their backs, and food on the table. There was no male figure around for them to communicate with, or to speak of showing them any love; God knows those are things every boy needs. I think sometimes even more than girls; because a girl most times has a mother she can talk openly with or should I say; it used to be that way more than it is today. However a father is really needed in the home unless there is a serious problem whereas there is more confusion and danger than safety for the entire family. My heart went out for some of these young men even though they did not know me. I truly believe that God always has a ram in the bush, someone watching you that you are not aware of or that you would least expect to care about you. Well I was one of those people (rams) who cared and I am glad about it. I saw where a barber school would be an asset to many talented young men and women and I went to God in prayer about a barber school. He had already opened the doors for me because at that time if the other school had not moved to another location there was something about the zoning law I was told that would have prevented me from opening Ea La Mar's Barber College in November 1989. As far as I knew and was told, this was the first female owned barber school, first single female owned barber school and first African American owned barber school in a number of states. Now keep in mind I said that I knew of. I'm sure there were some previously owned and operated by husbands or perhaps barber schools that had been left from broken marriages and other situations, but that's not what I'm saying here. I'm talking about starting from ground level up and as I think about how it was once a male dominated field. I would like to hear other female stories of how they started a barber school and how they managed to maintain it before the eighties. That would be interesting. I believe that if you had a husband, son, brother, uncle or any male working by your side then that was a game changer and again just remember we are not talking about a beauty school. I remember there were several beauty schools in different parts of the city when I opened my beauty school, but there were no female owned or operated barber schools. Now I know there will be many beauty school owners saying, we always did barbering in our beauty shops and beauty schools, and that's true; however, it is not quite the same thing. Before the barber school opened, I never would have thought anyone would have been against a trade that was so badly needed. The training of young men and women and a service for an entire community would benefit from such a venture. The trouble I encountered from all kinds of people did not surprise me as much as the trouble my own race (African Americans) demonstrated toward me. It lasted a long while and only God's help was sufficient to see me through. I was also told by one barber school owner, we don't want you, we don't need you and I want you to know I will be watching your every move. When I picked up on his attitude I told him, that's exactly what I want you to do and watch me lead you straight to Jesus. That was offensive to me especially being on a long distance call which I had made thinking this would be good news to him to some degree only to find out I was mistaken. Bets were made that I couldn't get the school opened. Some were saying that the man who owned the building that I was going to use for the barber school would have to get it opened for me and of course there were hundreds of other reasons that I would not be able to open a barber school. I was told by some older barbers that it had been tried before by Master Barbers and they couldn't do it. I remember telling an older barber that all of what they were saying was probably true but that I knew a Man and this older man asked me, what man? I told him the man I knew was named Jesus and that He could do anything but fail. That didn't make sense to him so he just played me off saying, we are talking real lady, not God talk. I knew I was talking real talk and I knew why I was going to do what had not been done. Sometimes people may be blocked because of their motives for doing things. I desired to help as many men and women become self-supportive as I could with a trade that would not only be beneficial but they also desired. For several months we did notice men casually well dressed coming into the school for haircuts. A few had on suits. It was obvious. They were not going to be regular customers; however they were nice and since we gave service to all it wasn't a problem for us. It only proves whatever door God opens, man cannot close it. That however does not keep them from trying.

My heart went out for young men, already cutting hair at home, which desired to be licensed. All they required was affordable tuition, knowledge and understanding of the trade, and someone to believe in them. There is no limit to how long or how much they can work or make just by adding their artistic ability to the field. I've found that young people are very talented, smart and unafraid to do constructive things if they have someone showing real interest in them and encouraging them. They sometimes have odd ways of showing their appreciation just as others sometimes do. If you continue to praise them and let them know you believe in them, an awful lot of times you will see them glowing and growing and that's what I look for and truly love. After a certain point they will continue to climb without an awful lot of pushing. I truly saw a need and when I got the barber school open I was thinking it would be such an asset, that it would certainly be highly appreciated. I guess to some it has been but there was trouble on every hand from the inside and outside. Some of the students would come to class and tell me what their barber had said and most times it was negative, however they didn't know or see what I knew and saw about my silent partner.

"I took what they were saying and used the negatives as a positive and kept climbing."

You see some of them were telling the students that they did not need a kit to work from and they did not need rollers and the things that came in their kits. So I told one young man that was so determined to do as his barber was telling him to do, I told him to give me back the kit and go enroll in his barber school. I tell you that I never had to say anything else to that young man but the next morning when school opened his mom was there to talk to me about allowing him to get back in school. She stated that she had been talking with him about his mouth and told him to close it. She stated she felt now he understood what she meant and that she was paying for his schooling not his barber. She asked if I would please allow him to return to school. She said she would be so grateful. Well by me being a mother trying to raise children by myself my heart certainly went out and still goes out for mothers. Our sons often times try to identify with a male and there's nothing wrong with that as long as the male they are listening to or trying to take patterns after mean well. However there are times we need to weigh what a person is saying to us and why, which is what most young people don't do. Because of his mother he did get back in school and the interesting thing about this case was when he was younger I understand that he had to go to a special school. Learning was somewhat a problem and he needed special help. That was not a real problem I felt, because I enjoy helping people who desire and are determined to learn, do just that. I can tell you he did learn. He passed the State

Board exam the first time and he is a wonderful barber. He was more than pleased with himself and I was equally pleased for him. I can remember a beauty student that said at the end of her training that she had learned more there than she learned in all of her years of school. Still another student said that now after finishing barber school he knew he could surely go on to college. Now some have gone on to college and I'm all for that because I feel if you never need to get another job, you can use education anywhere at any time for any purpose even to the point as just knowing you did finish for self-improvement and satisfaction. I recall several years after opening the barber school I would receive letters from men who were serving time wanting to know if I would accept them in the school after they got out and wanted information on the school because they had heard of the school. I sent information to them a few times but there was one young man in particular. He did not write for information, he sent his wife to talk with me. When she came to the school, introduced herself, and told me her husband asked her to talk with me about him attending barber school when he got out of prison and that wouldn't be long. It took her longer to make me realize who she was talking about than to give her an answer because it had been years since I last saw that young man. At one time we were members of the same church but at that time he had not entered his teens as I recall or I should say I didn't think he had entered his teen years; however, he was always a very pleasant, joyful and respectful young man and I sent word to him that I would certainly accept him in the barber school. Some months later I looked up from my desk and who did I see walking in to the school but him and I was glad to see him. I was determined to help him regardless of his situation. I accepted him in the barber school and he turned out to be a very good self-supportive barber and also an ordained minister. This should make us wonder who are we to say what another person can or should do. Isn't that God's job? Our real job is to pray and see what God has to say, as we look for a ways to help others and not just ourselves.

12

IF GOD ORDAINED IT HE WILL SUSTAIN IT

As I prepared for opening a school after finishing my own education, I had to use what had been put aside for my children's education (which wasn't much according to the full cost of a college education) but it was enough to get a good start. There was one time as usual, I looked up and already in the school door were Inspectors from the State Board. Now this was not unusual or a big surprise. Their job is to inspect schools and barber shops routinely. I was always fine with this. I never liked jumping or running when certain people showed up at any time or place. I like staying as ready as I can because it's better for everyone I feel. This particular time I think there were three Inspectors; two men and one woman. I don't know whether they had gotten on her last nerve or she was just having a bad day because out of my many years of dealing with Inspectors I can truly say ninety-eight percent of them have always been nice. This time she was different and angry. Even worse she had been one of the Inspectors that had been in the school before several times. This time she told me that I had to prove to the State Board that I could afford the barber school and I could not use cars, houses or collateral and I had to have the proof in to the office by the coming Monday; and this was told to me on a Friday. When she first started talking I started wondering what was going on but I just said, Ok. What ticked me off was that she then said to me, DO YOU UNDERSTAND?

That's when my Ok, played out and I let her know I heard her and that was all that was necessary and I was not about to take a lecture from her. I turned around and called the State Board and explained the things she had said as well as her attitude (especially with this not being my first and only school.) I was very stunned at the outcome because the State Board cleared this matter up very fast and told me there was no need for that proof and told me not to bother with the task.

"Remember, no obstacle is too big for God not even representatives of state licensing boards or anyone else. Who can withstand Our Great God?"

13

IMPORTANT MOMENTS

I have been able to share so many moments with many students. The fruits of my labor have enabled many a young person to support their families, become pillars in the community and provide a better quality of life for themselves. I'd like to take time to share some of the special and important moments, conversations and reflective words that students have shared with me to make my work meaningful.

Ms Mac,

Not only did you teach me more about what I love to do but you taught me more about keeping my focus on God. You also taught us that through all the good and bad times, to turn to God first. May God continue to bless you and Ea La Mar's. I will never forget you and what you have done in my life. Not only have your teachings helped me as a professional, but as a husband, as a father and as a Christian. Also as a young black man, to strive for greatness in all I do. I promise to make you and God proud. Thank you for all you have done. Matthew 28:20 says *"Teach them to obey everything that I have taught you, and I will be with you always, even until the end of this age."* And may God continue to be with you and your family.

-Sincerely with Love, Simmons 2006

Ms Mac,

How can I ever thank you? Thanks for the great insight about life, business, prayer...Thank you so much.

-Terry 2001

Ms Mac,

Thank you so much for all the teaching and encouraging words you gave me, and the having faith when my faith was growing low. I thank you from my heart.

-B. Crawford Jr. God bless you!

Ms Mac

You are a teacher who never gives up on a student. I'm glad about that. Teachers should have contagious enthusiasm and if they don't, you can rest assured that whatever they have, it is also contagious.

-S. M James

Ms Mac,

You are an inspiring young lady, mentor and spiritual person. You have designed EA LA MAR's Beauty and Barber College to prepare a student not only with skills; but with the business side of the hair industry too. You demanded discipline! At times, you ran the classroom like a boot camp. Playing games were out, while at the same time you managed to maintain respect for each student with a touch of humor. You are loaded with excellent qualities that tend to rub off on others and me. You have touched many people's lives, especially men who strive to get their lives together from low points in their lives. Thank you Mrs. McDonald for all that you have taught me and have a Happy New Year...

Yours Truly

-A. McGowin

Ms Mac,

You are a very good teacher that really is One of a kind. You have helped thousands of people who desire to make something of themselves.

-D. Durham

Ms Mac,

I thank God for inspiring you to do what you have done. You are a pillar in the community, a very knowledgeable, persistent, and wise teacher who has inspired a countless number of human beings with a spiritual base and teaching and the skills to master a trade which is very important to our community. You have been a pioneer in the industry and community. I am also thankful that you put God first in everything you did and led by example to put God first in everything. Going to school at Ea La Mar's allowed me to become a professional barber stylist, allowed me to meet my wife and led to me being able to become a man, a husband and eventually led to me becoming a father of two beautiful

young ladies. I'm always grateful that the professional and life skills I learned while with you continue to carry and support my family. Thank you so much for listening to God's voice and following his direction.

-Sincerely Yusef Harris

Ms Mac,

I can carry the ball myself now!

-Love N. PC   P.S. Thanks for the love and support

I want everyone to know there is a God. My life was a roller coaster ride for 15 years. I was smoking weed and drinking and using crack cocaine for a long time and that caused me to go to jail often. I started to go to AA, NA, and CA group meetings for nearly a year. I started working a couple of jobs and got hurt on one of them and had to stop working. My parents knew of Ms Mac's barber college and wanted me to meet her. I did meet her and I also told her that I did not have

any money but wanted to be a barber. She said come on and that my desire was what was important and we would work it out. She sent me to vocational rehabilitation. She told me what God could do. By the Grace of God, I am now a licensed barber and I have been clean and sober for 12 years. I thank God for Ms Mac.

-S. B.

In 1986, I was sentenced to 15 years in state prison. I stayed there 10 years and occupied my time by studying, going to school and trying to turn my life around. Trouble is so easy to get in yet so hard to get out of. Upon my release, Ms Mac blessed me with the opportunity to go to Ea La Mar's Barber School. It totally changed my life. Ms Mac and her staff will work with anyone that wants to change their lives. The barber school gives you a chance to get a trade to make a living and to be a role model for the younger guys. Ms Mac also introduced me to the Lord. If the Lord strengthens me as I know He can, I would love to return to finish my dream of getting my instructor's license and beautician's license. Thank you so much Ms Mac.

-Mr. J.

From the **"Whose That Lady"** Semi-Retirement Ceremony held at The Little Theater, Downtown, Kansas City, Missouri, April 4th. 2013

I would like to thank the Ea La Mar's staff – current and alumni, students, family, and friends for the outpouring of love on April 14th, 2013. There is a love that is far greater and stronger than the definition of the word. It is God's love that He gave me to use on you. For a long time I didn't understand it all, I only knew that I loved God's people (regardless). The good thing about this love is there is nothing anyone can do about it. Thank you all for a beautiful Salute (semi-retirement celebration – from 1982-2013) and I don't feel NO WAYS TIRED!! From the limousine ride, the awesome sounds by the band Oasis, to the closing of the night, I have not seen or enjoyed anything more. To anyone that I did not personally thank, here it is, THANK YOU, THANK YOU, THANK YOU! God's Love and mine Ms Mac.

"If God did not say It is impossible then, you cannot give up, give in or give out. Be well prepared so that when He opens that door you are well qualified by Him to walk through it. Obeying Him has helped welfare moms, street walkers, doubters, the falsely accused, the misunderstood, those hurt, disgusted, and abandoned men and women to become self-supporters, citizens, educators, and ministers which prove He can do anything but fail.

With God's Love and Mine,
Mrs. Shirley McDonald

She never let the negative comments stop her and there were many. *One master barber* *told her that setting up a barber school could not be done. He said others had tried it years ago and were blocked. And I would only be allowed to get an instructor's license but not a school. He made a bet with me that if I got a school, he would teach for me "free" because the only way I could get a school was if a "certain" man would help me get it. I told him that the man I know made the man that he was* *talking about. He made the mistake of asking "WHO?" I told him His name is Jesus. This was unexpected to him so he said "Oh Ms Mac, I'm taking about real things now. I took the bet. Later when the barber school was opened in 1989, I could not wait to tell him to come down so he could do some teaching for me. The look on his face was priceless. He could not teach "legally" because he did not have an instructor's license but he was a Master Barber and a very kind and helpful person. He only smiled and hugged me.*

An older business man *told me by phone shortly after opening the barber school "Lady, you have done a remarkable thing but I just want you to know you are in a "den of snakes." I told him that I really appreciated knowing that but God was in the den with me. From that day, I never heard anything else from him.*

Shirley McDonald - CEO & Founder

Ea La Mar's Beauty & Barber College

"If He did it for me – He is waiting to do it for you."

PROFILE OF INSPIRATION

Shirley McDonald (affectionately known as Ms Mac) is the CEO and Founder of Ea La Mar's Beauty and Barber College located in Kansas City, Missouri. She opened the beauty college in 1982 and the barber college in 1989. She has an impressive alumnus of profitable salon and barber shop owners. She has the distinguished honor of being the 1st Single African American female Barber School owner across several states. She instructs students from all lifestyles in cosmetology, barber, manicuring, & instructor's training. Along with her expertise in the beauty industry, she is provides her students counseling in all facets of starting and maintaining a growing and stable business.

Ms Mac has a passion for education. She has earned a Bachelor of Arts degree from University of Missouri, Kansas City; completed coursed at the Dale Carnegie School of business; attended Western Bible, Faith Bible, and Heart of America Bible colleges. She is currently working on her doctorate degree at the Western Baptist Bible College, Kansas City, MO. She has been a certified member of the Association of Scriptural Psychology Therapist recognized as a Certified Christian Counselor for several years. Ms Mac has obtained numerous awards and certificates in the field of cosmetology. One such award was given to her at the National Cosmetology Convention. Both state and national representatives competed for the Better Speaker contest. Shirley was first place winner in both categories.

Before opening her own school, she taught at numerous beauty schools throughout the Kansas City Metro area as well as Vocation Tech and Herndon in Lee's Summit, Missouri. Additionally, her credentials include a cosmetology license, a barber license, a barber's instructor's license, and a cosmetology instructor's license. She currently owns a barber and beauty school and once owned two daycare centers.

Ms Mac has taught at the Valerie Hurd Beauty College in Marshall Texas; Ailene Jefferson Beauty College, Kansas City, Mo; Lee Crawford Beauty Academy, Kansas City, MO; and, Paris Harrington, Kansas City, MO.

Ms Mac sponsored a radio program for five years on KGGN Radio entitled "Addicted to His Promises." The Kansas City Star newspaper has done two feature stories on Shirley entitled "Hope and a Haircut." The school opened to give young people hope that they could succeed and to offer barber and beauty services to an underserved neighborhood.

She is a people person and imparts her trust in God, passion for excellence, and zeal to succeed in every one she meets. At Ea La Mars, she aptly functions as Coordinator, Motivator, Mentor, and Enforcer. Shirley is tough but fair. She not only educates but she builds character in her students.

Ms Mac is a woman of faith and this book is her testimony of how faith will work for you when faced with overwhelming and seemingly impossible barriers.

PRAYER OF SALVATION

Perhaps you are reading this book and have not accepted Jesus the Christ as your Lord and Savior? I did and it was the best decision of my life. Soon after heeding the call from the Lord to ***come unto Him***, I began to hear his voice and understand that He was calling me into His Service. The bible promises "*That if thou shalt confess with thy mouth the Lord Jesus, and shalt believe in thine heart that God hath raised him from the dead, thou shalt be saved.*" *(Romans 10:9)*

It really is very simple. Pray this prayer from your heart and receive Jesus right where you are.

Dear Jesus, I believe that you died for me and that you rose again on the third day. I confess with my mouth that I am a sinner. I need Your love and Your forgiveness. Come into

my heart and forgive me of all my sins. I receive Your peace, joy and transforming love. Amen!

Now dear one get a good bible. Allow the Lord to lead you to a place of worship where you can work out your own soul salvation and God's predestined plan for your life. Be faithful to prayer and personal time with the Lord. Obey and accept the teaching from the pastor that God leads you to and GROW IN GRACE!

WELCOME TO THE FAMILY!

How To Purchase Products

Amazon

www.eagleseypressllc.com

Write To Us

shirlmac7@att.net

drmcw52@sbcglobal.net

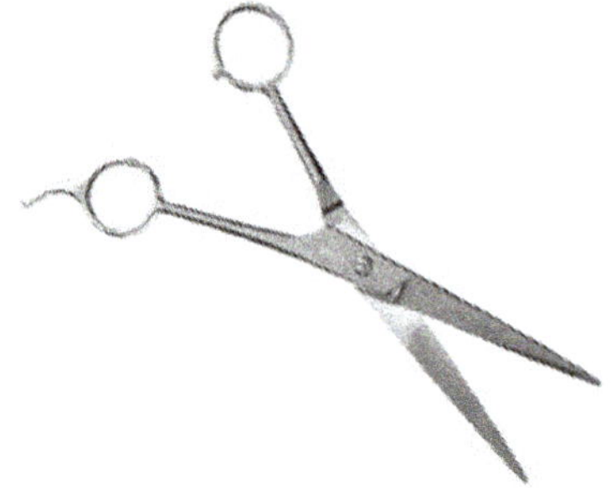

Alumni Remarks: Ms Mac…You never give up on a student. And I'm glad about that. Teachers have contagious enthusiasm and if they don't you can rest assured that whatever they have, it is also contagious.

We want to hear from you. Please send your comments about this book to us in care of the address below. Thank you.

Eagles Eye Press LLC
P O Box 6485
Lees Summit, MO 64064

www.ingramcontent.com/pod-product-compliance
Lightning Source LLC
Chambersburg PA
CBHW071844200326
41519CB00016B/4225

* 9 7 8 0 6 9 2 5 6 5 6 3 6 *